Butterfly4Jesus

VANESSA SYLVESTER

Copyright © 2025 by Vanessa Sylvester

All rights reserved.

ISBN: 978-1-916691-82-7

Author services by Opulent Books: www.OpulentBooks.net

No part of this publication may be reproduced, distributed, or transmitted in any form or by any means, including photocopying, recording, or other electronic or mechanical methods, without the prior written permission of the publisher, except as permitted by copyright law. For permission requests, contact the author.

Scripture quotations marked NKJV are taken from the *New King James Version® (NKJV)*. Copyright © 1982 by Thomas Nelson. Used by permission. All rights reserved.

Scripture quotations marked *KJV* are from the *King James Version* (Public Domain).

Scripture quotations marked *NIV* are from the *Holy Bible, New International Version® (NIV®)*. Copyright © 1973, 1978, 1984, 2011 by Biblica, Inc.™ Used by permission. All rights reserved worldwide.

Scripture quotations marked *NLT* are from the *Holy Bible, New Living Translation*, copyright © 1996, 2004, 2015 by Tyndale House Foundation. Used by permission of Tyndale House Publishers, Inc., Carol Stream, Illinois 60188. All rights reserved.

Scripture quotations marked *ESV* are from the *Holy Bible, English Standard Version® (ESV®)*, copyright © 2001 by Crossway, a publishing ministry of Good News Publishers. Used by permission. All rights reserved.

Scripture quotations marked *J.B. Phillips* are from *The New Testament in Modern English* by J.B. Phillips. Copyright © 1960, 1972 by J.B. Phillips. Used by permission of Macmillan Publishing Co., Inc.

Scripture quotations marked *AMP* are from the *Amplified® Bible*, copyright © 1954, 1958, 1962, 1964, 1965, 1987 by The Lockman Foundation. Used by permission. www.Lockman.org

FOREWORD

This is my second book, Butterfly4Jesus.

What an amazing feeling to be able to share the love of Jesus Christ. In such a way as to help inspire people of all genders.

Allowing the Light of Jesus to shine in the hearts and minds of the readers. I am now learning to live my life without limitations.

Flying high above the storms that may arise. Storms are very uncomfortable to endure, yet they are necessary. (For "Growth and Development" be that Butterfly4Jesus shine on beloved) God is faithful to us in many ways. I can't even count them all, for they are so vast in nature. Thanks be to God, where all blessings flow. (2 Corinthians 13:14 NIV).

My prayer for anyone who reads this book is to place your confidence in the Creator God. (Genesis 1:1 KJV).

(Proverbs 3:5-6 NIV) Trust in the LORD with all your heart.

Table of Contents

1:	Birthing Process	1
2:	Cost of Freedom	11
3:	Limitations	17
4:	Maturity	25
5:	The Flight	31
6:	Hidden Dangers	37
7:	Covering	43

1

BIRTHING PROCESS

"Shall I bring to the time of birth, and not cause delivery?" says the Lord. "Shall I who cause delivery shut up the womb?" says your God."

Isaiah 66:9 (NKJV)

In any birth, there is always pain involved—whether physical, spiritual, or mental. Either way, your journey in life has begun. Taking your first breath is a mystery in itself. Only God can grant such a miraculous occurrence. To arrive on the path to greatness, one has to suffer loss.

Allow me to share a brief testimony. I remember enduring a lot of suffering when I was a child, not being able to enjoy my life fully because it was filled with poverty. Both of my parents were teenagers, 15 and 17 years of age. My father was an adulterous man, and my mother was very humble and meek. I can see how this dysfunction shaped and molded me in various ways. It taught me how to endure hardships as a good soldier of Jesus Christ. (2 Timothy 2:3 KJV). Building character and hope in a weary land. Might I say, this caused me to recognize the Lord's voice in Scripture.

You see, beloved! I accepted the Lord Jesus as my Lord and Savior at 8 years old. I knew enough of God's Holy Word to read it and be comforted. In the Book of Romans, it speaks of suffering.

(Romans 5:3-5 KJV) "Not only so, but we also glory in our sufferings, because we know that suffering produces perseverance; perseverance, character; and character, hope."

(2 Corinthians 4:16-18 KJV) states: "Therefore we do not lose heart. Though outwardly we are wasting away, yet inwardly we are being renewed day by day."

And lastly, (1 Peter 4:12 KJV) says: "Dear friends, do not be surprised at the fiery ordeal that has come on you to test you, as though something strange were happening to you."

This, my friend, is the beginning of the birthing forth. Will you embrace it or simply stand still like a mannequin on a showroom floor? Life is what you make out of it, believer.

Now let us talk about the "BIRTHING PROCESS." With it, you'll experience a metamorphosis. The definition of metamorphosis is a change in one's nature, being turned into a completely different person altogether. Whether it's by natural or supernatural means, change is inevitable either way. Birthing consists of these three components: **Transformation, Transfiguration, and Conversion.**

Transformation entitles a person to be totally changed into the image and likeness of Jesus Christ. This is called a "Spiritual Birth." You can read the story of Nicodemus in the gospel of John 3:1-36 KJV—an interesting story of one desiring change. Our Lord Jesus answered Nicodemus' question on how a man can be born again a second time. Do they enter back into their mother's womb? We see here that Jesus was speaking of spiritual birth, not physical, as Nicodemus' mind was leading him. Scripture states that if a man is not born again, he cannot enter into heaven. (John 3:3-7 NIV)

(Isaiah 55:8-9 NIV) reminds us that the Lord's ways are

not always made known to us at first sight. To be able to 'see' is one thing. To accurately 'know' and 'believe' is not the same in collation as a person often thinks. In order to see, one must look straightforward and stay with the proper perspective. In knowing, one has to obtain the knowledge for that task. Also, in believing, you cannot doubt in your heart—you must have faith. (Hebrews 11:1 NIV)

Let me share another testimony of my life being transformed. I can truly say I never knew how dark my life was until I met Jesus. I was baptized along with my first cousins in a Baptist Church in the 70s (Moses' Baptist Church). This is where I began to come alive inside my spirit. My grandmother would give us money to put in the offering on Sunday morning. Like children, we stopped on our way to church and bought candy, pickles, and chips, not being aware that the smell lingered on our breath and clothes. She was always watching at a distance, observing her grandchildren. I often felt guilty because it was wrong, and God was watching. Back then, I had a reverent fear of the Lord—and I still do today. My spiritual eyes were opened to my sin. I prayed silently, repenting and asking the Lord Jesus Christ to forgive me.

The next component I will dissect is **Transfiguration**. To transfigure, one must be fully surrendered to God Almighty—you see, it's a spiritual awakening. It is defined as a complete change of form or appearance into a more beautiful spiritual state. Nothing on this earth can give a person a greater awareness of this than God Himself.

Let us take a look at the transfiguration of the Lord Jesus Christ on the Mount of Transfiguration. Jesus' disciples were in absolute fear—this was something they had never seen before. (Moses, Elias, and Jesus all together in spiritual form, communicating). Wow! What a spectacular moment to encounter. The text is found in the gospels (Matthew 7:21, Mark 9:2-3, Luke 9:28-36 KJV).

Beloved, when you and I really leave this life of sin, we also will enter into this radiant form of transfiguration—total amazement to those who knew us before the new birth experience. Brilliantly shining for our Lord Jesus in the spiritual realm as well as on the earth. Now, we are becoming more like the Creator-being that Butterfly4Jesus transformed into His image and likeness. (2 Corinthians 3:18 NLT). Amen!

I have been transfigured into the likeness and image of our dear Savior, Jesus Christ. My life is filled with the light of

His glory, shining brightly for all the world to see. I cannot be hidden any longer. Hallelujah!

Scripture reference: "You are the world's light—it is impossible to hide a town built on the top of a hill. Men do not light a lamp and put it under a bucket. They put it on a lampstand and it gives light for everybody in the house." (Matthew 5:14-15, J.B. Phillips New Testament)

Beloved, we are written epistles read by men everywhere. The world is watching how we look and appear to them. Our light must continue to shine bright! (2 Corinthians 3:2 AMP) [No] you yourselves are our letter of recommendation (our credentials), written in your hearts, to be known (perceived, recognized) and read by everybody. Take note: Transfigured for the Lord's Glory.

Beloved, this leads us right to the last component—**Conversion**. In the process of changing, conversion has to happen inside our hearts first. Then, we are on our way to a life that is geared towards repentance. Without it, the new birth experience will not take place. (Matthew 18:3 NIV)

The Lord Jesus states this while being with His disciples at the Lord's Supper: how Satan desires to sift us as wheat. In the Gospel of Luke 22:31-32 NIV, it reads: "And the Lord said, Simon, Simon! Indeed, Satan has asked for you, that he may sift you as wheat."

At times, we are handed over to our adversary to be tested and tried—to reveal what has changed in us since we believed in Jesus Christ. I can honestly say I've been through many tests and trials in my life—tests of love, forgiveness, and temptation, particularly in the area of lust. You see, fornication runs deep in my bloodline—unwed pregnancies, whoremongering, and other struggles common to humanity. I'm not proud of it, but this has been the test the enemy often uses to throw me off track.

I thank God for Jesus and His saving grace through the redemptive power of the Cross of Calvary.

Beloved, let us consider 'conversion' from a different perspective. In the traditional message of Jesus Christ to a Spirit-filled believer, life was marked by transformation—often evidenced by speaking in tongues. Back then, conversion was a powerful, visible experience. Even today, it is spectacular to witness—men, women, boys, and girls receiving the precious gift of the Holy Spirit.

"And it will be in the last days," says God, "that I will pour out My Spirit on all humanity; then your sons and daughters will prophesy, your young men will see visions, and your old men will dream dreams." (Acts 2:17 NKJV). Hallelujah!

I remember childish laughter as the choir sang and the organist played old spirituals. My favorite song was *This Little Light of Mine, I'm Going to Let It Shine.* Thank God—I pray I keep that light shining throughout my life.

One powerful example of this great conversion is the Apostle Paul—formerly known as Saul of Tarsus (see Acts 8:1–3 and Acts 9:1–2, KJV). He was a fierce persecutor of the Jews who followed Jesus Christ, known then as followers of *the Way*. Saul was present at the stoning of Stephen—the devil truly had him blinded. But this was a pivotal moment in his life, because God had other plans.

That Damascus Road journey changed everything. Blinded by the enemy to do evil, Almighty God turned his blindness into light—into salvation through the Lord Jesus Christ. Glory to God!

"Freedom is never free—its cost is your surrender, your obedience, and sometimes, your very soul."

Vanessa Sylvester

2

COST OF FREEDOM

"Stand fast therefore in the liberty by which Christ has made us free, and do not be entangled again with a yoke of bondage."

Galatians 5:1 (NKJV)

By no means is freedom free. It will always cost you something. Whether spiritual, emotional, or physical, freedom comes with a price. We may desire it, shout for it, even pray for it, but are we truly ready to pay for it?

As we journey here on planet earth, mankind has always contended for freedom, and always will. From biblical days until now, humanity has cried out for liberty. Great battles have been fought for freedom. Blood has been shed, tears have been cried, and lives have been laid down just to secure what we often take for granted.

Take a look at our nation today—in a total uproar—all for the simple fact that people want to be free. Free from oppression. Free from injustice. Free from religious persecution. Free from being held hostage by the stigma of slavery, both natural and spiritual. But one might ask, *slave to what?*

People, places, and things in this world system have blinded the hearts and minds of mankind in general. The chains may not be visible, but they're real. Invisible shackles of fear, addiction, lust, greed, and sin grip the souls of many. Not taking a second glance at the cost, people chase what looks like freedom, only to discover it demands more than they imagined.

Let us not ignore the truth: such accomplishments hold a hefty price. And that, my dear brethren, is your very soul.

This is a war between immortality vs. mortality. Eternal life or eternal separation. The choice is yours.

(2 Chronicles 7:13–14 KJV) — "If my people, which are called by my name..." You know the rest.

Look at the history of the world we live in. Man is

constantly searching for a way to escape. Yes—escape! Escape the pressure, the pain, the brokenness, the guilt. Escape the reality of how sinful the environment of man has become. It is so toxic and polluted that its very stench causes one to vomit out the sin festering in the heart.

No wonder God chose Noah to build an ark made of gopher wood during his time. (Genesis 6:1–22 KJV). Humanity had fallen so far that only a faithful man, obedient to God's instruction, could become the channel for salvation. His obedience became the vehicle of deliverance.

Faithfulness, along with the Spirit of obedience, will win every time.

In one of the greatest defeats ever against our adversary—the devil—(John 10:10 KJV), our Lord and Savior Jesus Christ conquered death, hell, and the grave at Calvary's Cross over two thousand years ago.

He paid the ultimate cost. That, beloved, is the price tag on our freedom. Hallelujah!

Thank You, Father God, for sending us Your only begotten Son, Jesus, into the world to die for mankind.

(John 3:16 KJV).

This, my brethren, is the Cost of Freedom—exemplified beyond measure.

Amen!

Prayer: Lord Jesus, thank You for paying the ultimate price for my freedom. Help me never take it for granted. Teach me to walk in obedience, to stay clear of bondage, and to live boldly for You. Strengthen me to stand firm in the liberty You've given me, and guide me away from anything that would steal my soul's peace. In Your powerful name, Amen.

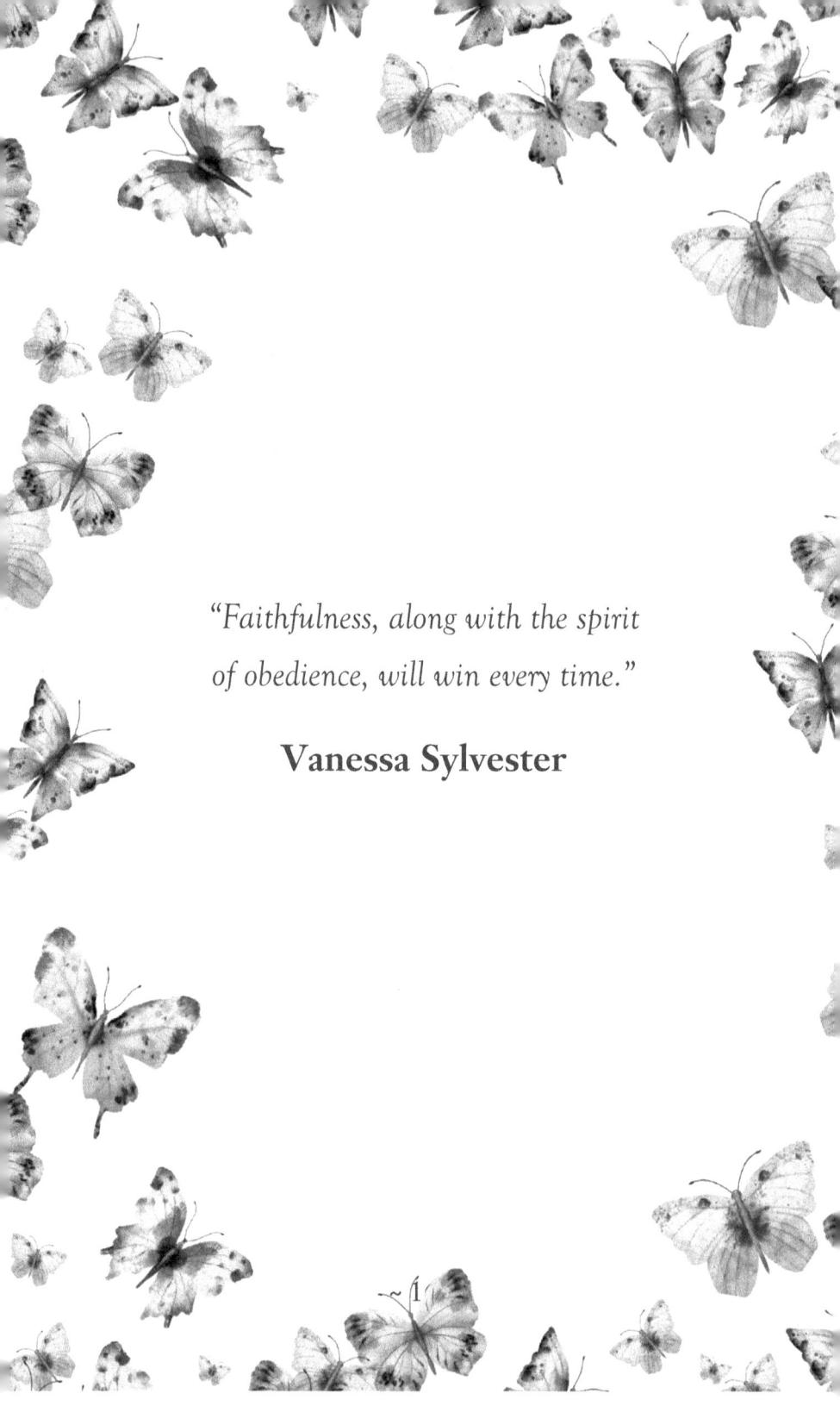

"Faithfulness, along with the spirit of obedience, will win every time."

Vanessa Sylvester

3

LIMITATIONS

"I can do all things through Christ who strengthens me."

Philippians 4:13 (NKJV)

Now, beloved, let us take a look at all the limitations we place on our lives.

The word *limitation* is defined as a restriction—a barrier, a ceiling, an invisible chain that keeps us from moving forward. How awful this is to the person who desires growth and purpose. Limitations destroy momentum, delay destiny, and derail the path toward future goals. They are subtle yet powerful, often hidden in thought patterns, past traumas, self-doubt, or spiritual strongholds. This word has many facets—each one carefully designed to cause a person to suffer loss, to break focus, and to abandon purpose.

Below are seven powerful attributes that expose the destructive nature of limitations—and how we must overcome them with the Word of God:

1. It Stagnates (No growth whatsoever)

Limitation arrests movement. It keeps a person stuck in the same place, year after year, season after season—with no visible change, no upward motion, and no advancement. Just like a seed that is never watered, potential remains buried. Dreams begin to rot beneath the surface. The person may still be breathing, but they're not truly living. Beloved, stagnation is not your portion. God desires that we move from Glory to Glory (2 Corinthians 3:18 KJV), growing in grace and in the knowledge of Him.

2. No Prosperity in Life

A limited mindset shuts the door to abundance. You cannot prosper in your body, finances, relationships, or purpose if you've already determined—even subconsciously—that it's not possible. The enemy wants to cut off your supply by convincing you that you're not worthy, not ready, or not able. But God's Word declares: "Beloved, I wish above all things that thou mayest prosper and be in health, even as thy soul prospereth." (3 John 1:2 KJV) Prosperity begins in the soul. When you are mentally and spiritually blocked, so is your harvest.

3. A Mind Adjustment Must Occur

(Proverbs 23:7 KJV) "For as he thinketh in his heart, so is he..." This is key. Your thoughts shape your reality. If you believe you are limited, you will behave as though you are. Your speech, decisions, and attitude will all reflect what you think about yourself, even if it's a lie. Beloved, God has not given you a spirit of fear, but of power, love, and a sound mind (2 Timothy 1:7 KJV). It's time to renew your mind daily with the truth of God's Word and take every limiting thought captive (Romans 12:2, 2 Corinthians 10:5 KJV). Freedom starts in the mind.

4. It Causes Failure (Dreams and hopes are hindered)

Limitation doesn't just delay dreams—it suffocates them. A person burdened by limitations may start projects but never finish. They dream big but speak small. They want to fly but clip their own wings with fear, regret, and doubt.

The Lord did not create us to live in cycles of failure. Through Christ, we are more than conquerors (Romans 8:37). But we must confront those invisible walls of limitation that hinder our God-given hopes from becoming reality.

5. No Stability (Don't be double minded, listening to the wrong voices for your life)

"A double minded man is unstable in all his ways." (James 1:8 KJV) One minute, you're on fire for your calling; the next, you're buried in insecurity. One day, you're walking in faith; the next, you're stuck in fear. This is what double-mindedness looks like—and it is rooted in limitation. It stems from listening to conflicting voices: the voice of the world, the opinions of people, and your own inner critic. The voice of God must be the loudest in your life. When your mind is anchored in truth, your life gains stability and direction.

6. Lack of Faith

(James 1:6 KJV) "But let him ask in faith, nothing wavering…" Without faith, it is impossible to please God. Limitation thrives where faith is weak. It tells you to play it safe, to settle for less, to stay in your comfort zone. But faith dares you to believe the impossible. It pushes past fear. It stretches you into purpose. If you lack faith, you remain bound. But if you have even mustard-seed faith, you can move mountains (Matthew 17:20 KJV). Today is the day to silence every voice of limitation and rise up in faith.

7. Must Be Able to Trust God Almighty Fully

"Trust in the Lord with all thine heart; and lean not unto thine own understanding." (Proverbs 3:5-7 KJV)
Trust is the antidote to limitation. When we fully trust God, not halfway, not just when things are easy, we give Him permission to move in power. Letting go of limitations means letting go of the need to control everything. It means believing that God knows best—even when the path is unclear. True freedom comes when you surrender your limitations and trust God completely.

Beloved, in order to end this dilemma of limitation, we must prosper and be in good health, even as our soul prospers (3 John 1:2 KJV). An unhealthy soul is one left in the dark, conformed to the world system, bound by fear and false identity.

But YOU, beloved, are not called to stay there. Why not take the limits off today, my dear brethren? So you can rise to the occasion of being a total success—not by the world's standards, but by heaven's measure. Just remember:

❋ **You are a Butterfly4Jesus**—even if you can't fully fathom it yet. You are simply beautiful—inside and out.

Prayer: *Lord, help me to break free from every limitation holding me back. Renew my mind, strengthen my faith, and teach me to trust You fully. I choose to rise and walk in the freedom You've given me. In Jesus' name, Amen.*

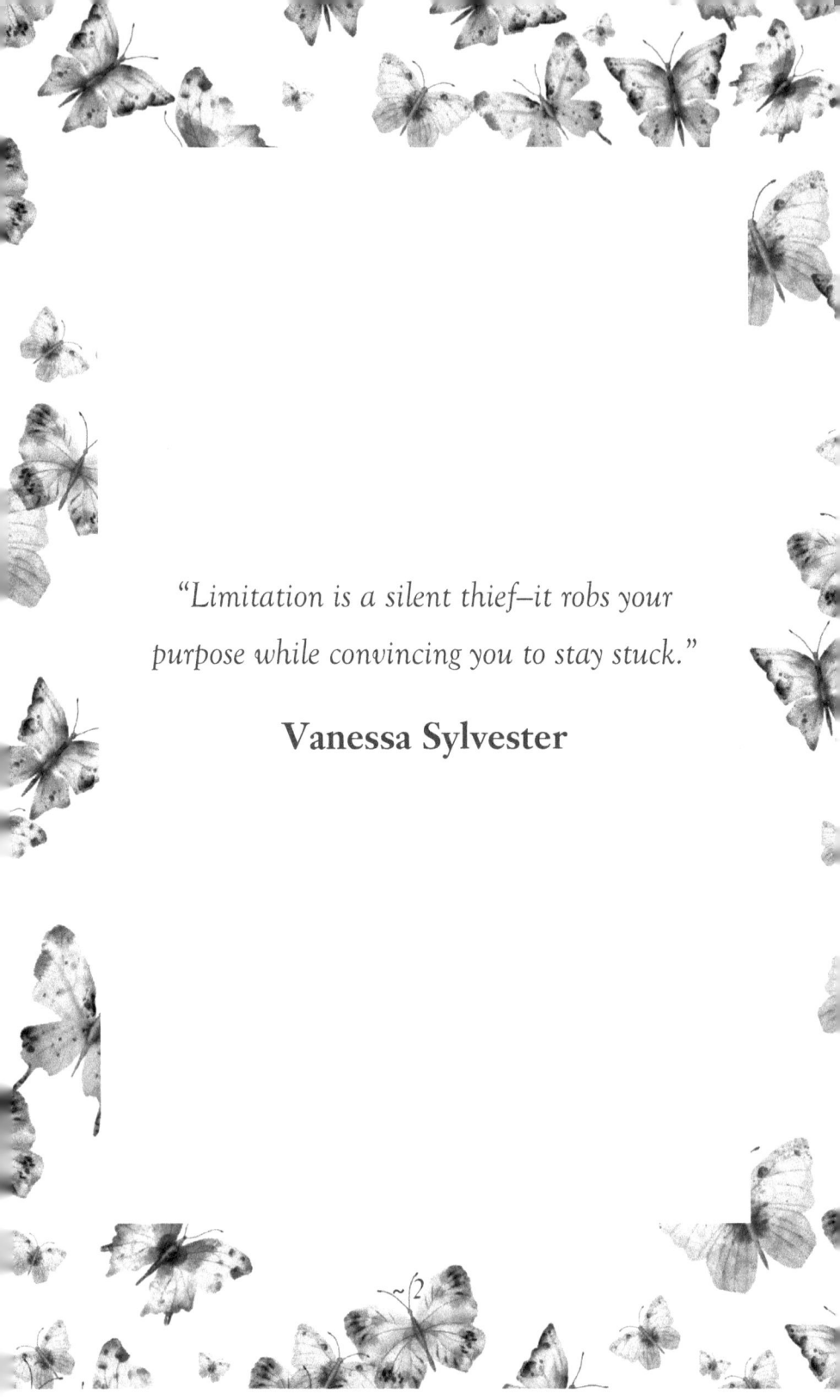

> "Limitation is a silent thief—it robs your purpose while convincing you to stay stuck."

Vanessa Sylvester

4

MATURITY

"He is the one we proclaim, admonishing and teaching everyone with all wisdom, so that we may present everyone fully mature in Christ."

Colossians 1:28 (NIV)

Maturity comes with growth—and an abundance of mistakes. If you think back on your childhood and adolescent years, the changes were very difficult. It's never easy trying to be an adult while exhibiting childlike behavior. That, beloved, is truly embarrassing to behold.

One must learn to break free of all obstacles blocking the maturity process. Below are key areas to evaluate when pressing toward spiritual and emotional growth:

1. Unhealthy Relationships (Block your view from moving forward)

I was in a few. They blocked my view from moving forward in life. They brought an unsettling to my Spirit—yet I pursued without cause or caution. My life became more difficult to bear. People who were once friends turned into mere enemies. A love-to-hate relationship... what a dilemma to endure.

2. Bad Choices (Stop making foolish mistakes)

While examining my life, I see how many of my choices were not good. I can't even remember all the bad decisions I made. They caused delay after delay. I wasn't progressing—I was standing still in one position. I often wonder; What was I thinking during those seasons of my life?

I became corrupt in my daily habits—living in fornication at times. I even thought about getting out, but fear and embarrassment gripped my heart. Eventually, I moved on with my life and stopped making those foolish mistakes.

3. Sacrifice (Sleepless nights)

To follow the law of Jesus, one must make sacrifices in order to survive. Oh yes, beloved, there will be many sleepless nights. The sinful nature must die immediately. Although the layers of the past are removed one at a time, it takes work, beloved of God. Let the pruning process begin.

4. Boldness (Maintaining your vision)

Be bold. Be strong, for the Lord thy God is with you. So often, we think we are on this journey alone—but lo and behold, we are not! The Lord Jesus left the gift of the Holy Spirit for you and me, dwelling within our hearts and our very being. This, my dear brethren, sustains your vision and strengthens your journey to maturity.

5. Focus-Driven (The only way to conquer)

One must be so driven by one's destiny that moving backward is not even an option. Remember the vision of a raging bull—his only objective is the target.

Here's another example, beloved of God: a runner on the track field. One sprints, another runs the long jump, and another takes the high jump. Yet they all have one thing in common—focus. Their goal is to finish the race completely.

6. Be Open to Growth (Learn new things, broaden your horizon)

Learning new ways, new ideas, and new avenues—it matters. Growth requires us to broaden our horizons. Join a study group. Find godly mentorship. It is vital to your development in the things of God.

Surround yourself with positive, successful people and mirror their teachings. As you do this, beloved, you'll begin to notice the changes happening rapidly.

Scripture to glean from is (1 Corinthians 13:11 ESV): "When I was a child, I spoke like a child, I thought like a child, I reasoned like a child. When I became a man, I gave up childish ways."

What about you and me? Are we going to learn these valuable truths or stay as babies in Christ Jesus, never able to digest the meat of the Word of God? Simply remaining stuck in a cycle of disbelief in a world that is constantly evolving around us. (1 Corinthians 3:1-3 KJV)

Prayer: *Heavenly Father, I know You chose me to be light. As Your daughter, I want to be a beacon of light for others who need it. May they see You inside me. May this light You gave me help others to draw closer to You. In Jesus name, Amen.*

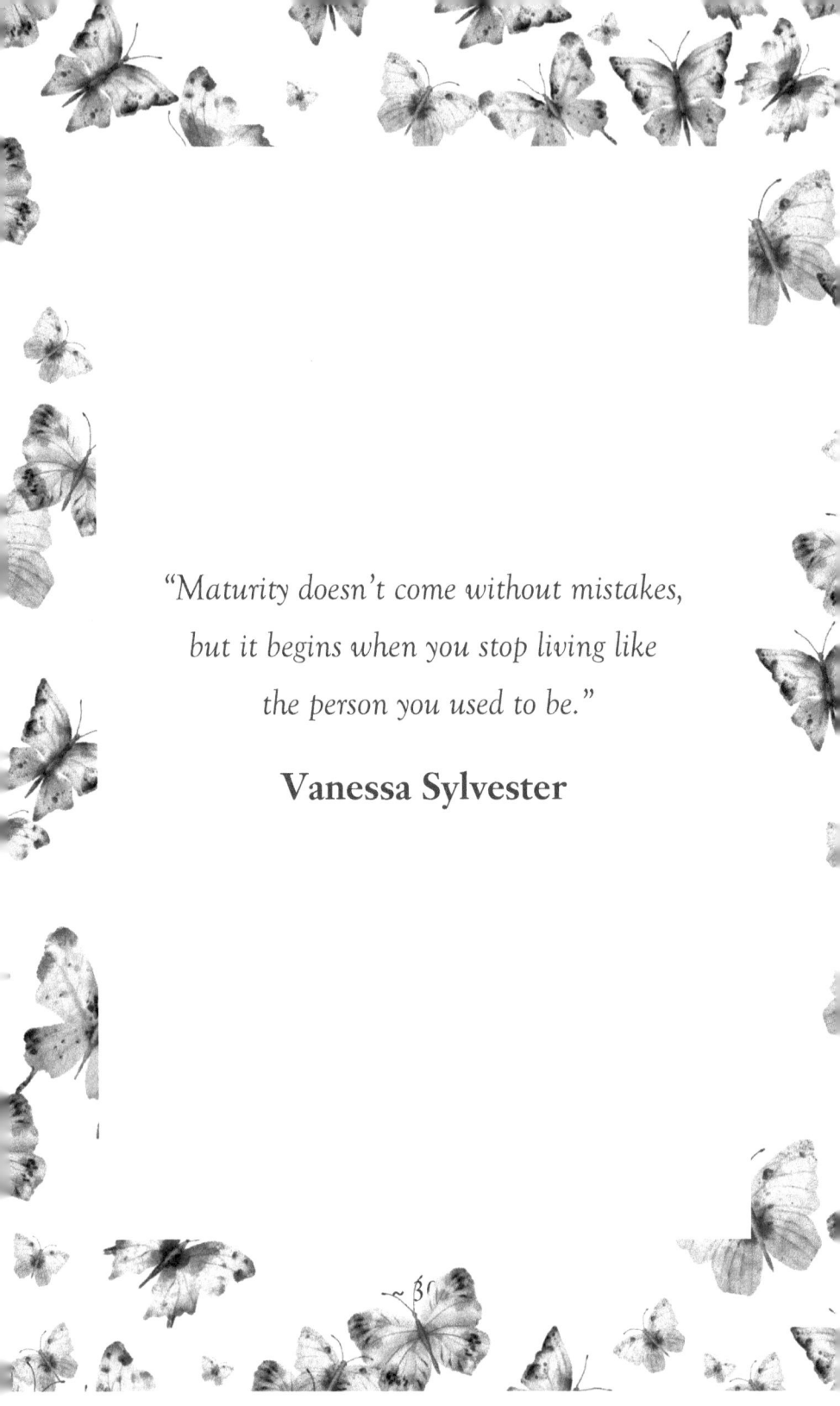

"Maturity doesn't come without mistakes, but it begins when you stop living like the person you used to be."

Vanessa Sylvester

5

THE FLIGHT

"But those who wait on the Lord shall renew their strength; they shall mount up with wings like eagles, they shall run and not be weary, they shall walk and not faint."

Isaiah 40:31 (NKJV)

In being a Butterfly4Jesus, our flight is everything. Taking off requires precise skill when lifting up from ground level. It's not a simple leap—it's a carefully guided elevation. As we rise, we maneuver with grace and intention, causing onlookers to take notice.

They see the shift. They notice our posture. Something's different. We are no longer seated—we're poised for takeoff. No longer bound by the old place. Ready for launch at any given moment. And once the wings stretch open, an upward bound is all that matters now.

But hear this, beloved: In flight, one must be able to navigate the atmosphere. Altitudes shift. Winds blow. Distractions come. And so, a mature flyer must be equipped with spiritual focus and discernment. Below are essential truths every Butterfly4Jesus must remember on this divine flight of destiny.

1. Steady the Course

Don't waver. Don't be tossed by every wind of emotion or opinion. When turbulence hits, stay steady. Remain consistent in prayer, in praise, and in your identity. This is your flight. Don't let fear knock you off course.

2. Know Your Navigational Ordinances Before You Take Flight

These ordinances give clear direction, steering you to your appointed destination. They are your spiritual flight map—rooted in God's Word. Caution: Don't go blindly into things. Preparation and prayer must come before elevation.

The Flight

3. You May or May Not Have a Destination in Mind

If you do—chart it first. Write it down on paper. Picture it in your mind. Is the image clearer now? If so, proceed further. Get excited because you're getting ready for takeoff. Your life has begun afresh.

If not, please stay seated until the time is right for you. Every season has a window for departure. Wait on the Lord to release you.

4. Who is on Board?

You must know who is among you. On this new journey in life, it's vital to know their names, occupations, and, most importantly, if they love Jesus. Are they led by the Spirit, or they are sent to bring distractions?

In the world, people say, "Who you riding with?" As born-again believers, we must ask the same. Know your passengers. Know your people. This awareness could literally save your life.

5. Hand Out and Give Instructions for a Safe Landing

Inform people what to expect while flying with Jesus. Let them know—this is a faith flight. High altitudes bring turbulence—knocks, bumps, and resistance on the Christian journey.

It won't always be easy. Stay calm. Don't panic. Keep pressing forward. In the pressing, the landing becomes smoother. The knockdowns lessen. Even the bumps on the road to daily living become fewer.

6. Welcome Them Onboard

Welcome those who choose to ride this journey with you. I hope to see you again soon. Please share with your family and friends how to land safely until their next venture in life.

Be watchful of who you take with you into any new season that God calls you to. This will make all the difference in the world. Believe me, I've been there.

Scripture reference: (Proverbs 3:5-7 KJV) In reaching higher in life, remember to always let God be the pilot, for He is the one who is guiding the wheel. Amen!

Prayer: Lord, lift me higher. Teach me how to fly with grace and purpose. Show me how to discern the right time to take off and the right people to bring on board. Help me navigate the winds of life with faith and focus. I surrender control and trust You to be the pilot of this flight. In Jesus' name, Amen.

*"Every season has a window for departure
—wait on the Lord to release you."*

Vanessa Sylvester

6

HIDDEN DANGERS

"And no wonder! For Satan himself transforms himself into an angel of light. Therefore it is no great thing if his ministers also transform themselves into ministers of righteousness..."

2 Corinthians 11:14–15 (NKJV)

So, the flight has landed safely. We are now back on the ground. But beloved, don't relax just yet. Now it's time to prepare ourselves, because not every danger is visible during the flight. Some are waiting for us when we land.

There are hidden dangers all around us—traps set to sabotage your calling. These are not always obvious. Sometimes, they're dressed in religious clothing. This is why Jesus warned us about the leaven of the Pharisees and

Sadducees—the false doctrine that creeps into the Church and corrupts the soul (Matthew 16:6, 11–12; 2 Timothy 3:5–7, 14–17 KJV).

This kind of deception will ruin your spiritual life and shake your foundation. It keeps your roots from growing deep into good soil (Matthew 13:1–23; Mark 4:8; Luke 8:15 KJV). If our Lord Jesus hadn't warned us about these dangers ahead of time, we would have been left vulnerable. But praise God—He reveals so we can be ready.

Below are six hidden dangers that every believer must watch for:

1. Wolves in Sheep's Clothes (Matthew 7:15 KJV)

They are all around us. Our churches are under attack from this evil villain, lurking among the true sheep of God's fold, waiting to strike at any time.

Even during the time of Jesus, there were plenty of them. So-called men and women pretending to follow Christ. They blended in easily, fleecing the Lord's sheep. Only in it for money, they captivated the hearts and minds of the unsuspecting. Be alert.

2. The Spirit of Pride (1 John 2:16; Proverbs 16:18 KJV)

A showmanship attitude to gain attention. My God—high and mighty, always on top. The 'Look at me' Spirit. High. Puffed up. Proud. Arrogant. It's all about them. Pride comes before destruction and a haughty spirit before a fall.

3. Do Not Be Led Astray (Jeremiah 50:6 KJV)

As followers of Jesus, we must be careful who we follow. Sheep are often led astray by charismatic leaders with loud voices—but empty vessels. Beloved, know the Word for yourself. Test every Spirit. Don't be deceived.

4. Being Tossed to and Fro (Ephesians 4:14 KJV)

Stop running from prophet to prophet, apostle to apostle, trying to hear the voice of God. Know God for yourself. The Spirit of deception is rampant today. Lights. Camera. Action. It's showtime—but where is the Spirit of the Lord?

Many are power-struck, not Spirit-led. Stay rooted. Stay grounded in truth.

5. Hiding Iniquity Inside Your Heart (Psalm 66:18; Matthew 3 KJV)

My God! The Word says if you hide iniquity in your heart, your prayers won't be heard. What a dilemma to have. A person can preach the gospel while still living in sin. That's the danger of iniquity—it distorts your character. Lust and inordinate affection are disgusting, especially when directed toward the people of God. It gives the Church a black eye. That's why so many reject Jesus today.

6. Love Thy Neighbor (Matthew 5:43; 22:39; Galatians 5:14; James 2:8 KJV)

We are commanded to love our neighbor as ourselves, not to bring pain and suffering. Beloved, this should not be.

Love like Jesus—unconditionally. Remember, this is the first commandment with a promise. Let love be your protection and your proof.

By heeding these warnings from Father God, we can avoid many pitfalls and preserve our spiritual integrity. These are the hidden dangers that quietly erode purpose if ignored. A word for the wise: (Proverbs 4:7 KJV) "Wisdom is the principal thing; therefore get wisdom: and with all thy getting, get understanding." Amen!

Prayer: Father, open my eyes to see clearly. Help me discern what is real from what is false. Expose every hidden danger around me and guard my heart from deception. Keep me rooted in Your truth and filled with Your Spirit. Teach me to love like Jesus and live with integrity. In Jesus' name, Amen.

Not every danger is visible during the flight —some are waiting when you land."

Vanessa Sylvester

7

COVERING

"And there will be a tabernacle for shade in the daytime from the heat, for a place of refuge, and for a shelter from storm and rain."

Isaiah 4:6 (NKJV)

To remain a Butterfly4Jesus, we must have a covering so strong that the enemies of this world won't be able to destroy us. Hallelujah! We are truly covered under the shadow of Almighty God, day and night. Psalm 91:1–16 KJV is a beautiful reminder of His divine protection over humanity:

He who dwells in the secret place of the Most High
Shall abide under the shadow of the Almighty.

I will say of the Lord, "He is my refuge and my fortress;
My God, in Him I will trust."

Surely, He shall deliver you from the snare of the fowler
And from the perilous pestilence.
He shall cover you with His feathers,
And under His wings you shall take refuge;

His truth shall be your shield and buckler.
You shall not be afraid of the terror by night,
Nor of the arrow that flies by day,
Nor of the pestilence that walks in darkness,
Nor of the destruction that lays waste at noonday.

A thousand may fall at your side,
And ten thousand at your right hand;
But it shall not come near you.
Only with your eyes shall you look,
And see the reward of the wicked.

Because you have made the Lord, who is my refuge,
Even the Most High, your dwelling place,
No evil shall befall you,
Nor shall any plague come near your dwelling;
For He shall give His angels charge over you,
To keep you in all your ways.

In their hands they shall bear you up,
Lest you dash your foot against a stone.
You shall tread upon the lion and the cobra,
The young lion and the serpent you shall trample underfoot.

"Because he has set his love upon Me, therefore I will deliver him;
I will set him on high,
Because he has known My name.
He shall call upon Me, and I will answer him;
I will be with him in trouble;
I will deliver him and honor him.
With long life I will satisfy him,
And show him My salvation."

He's like an umbrella that protects us from the rays of the hot sun and from the torrential rain that falls from the sky. We are covered completely, blocking every barrier the devil might try to build against mankind.

The Lord Jesus triumphantly defeated death, hell, and the grave upon that rugged Cross over two thousand years ago. Though the conditions were harsh and the suffering was beyond what we can imagine, He endured it all. He completed the task for you and for me.

So, beloved, let us become that Butterfly4Jesus, covering one another with the agape love of God.

Amen!

Prayer: Lord, thank You for being my covering and my refuge. Hide me under the shadow of Your wings and protect me from every plot of the enemy. Help me walk in the assurance that I am never alone. Teach me to extend that same covering love to others. In Jesus' name, Amen.

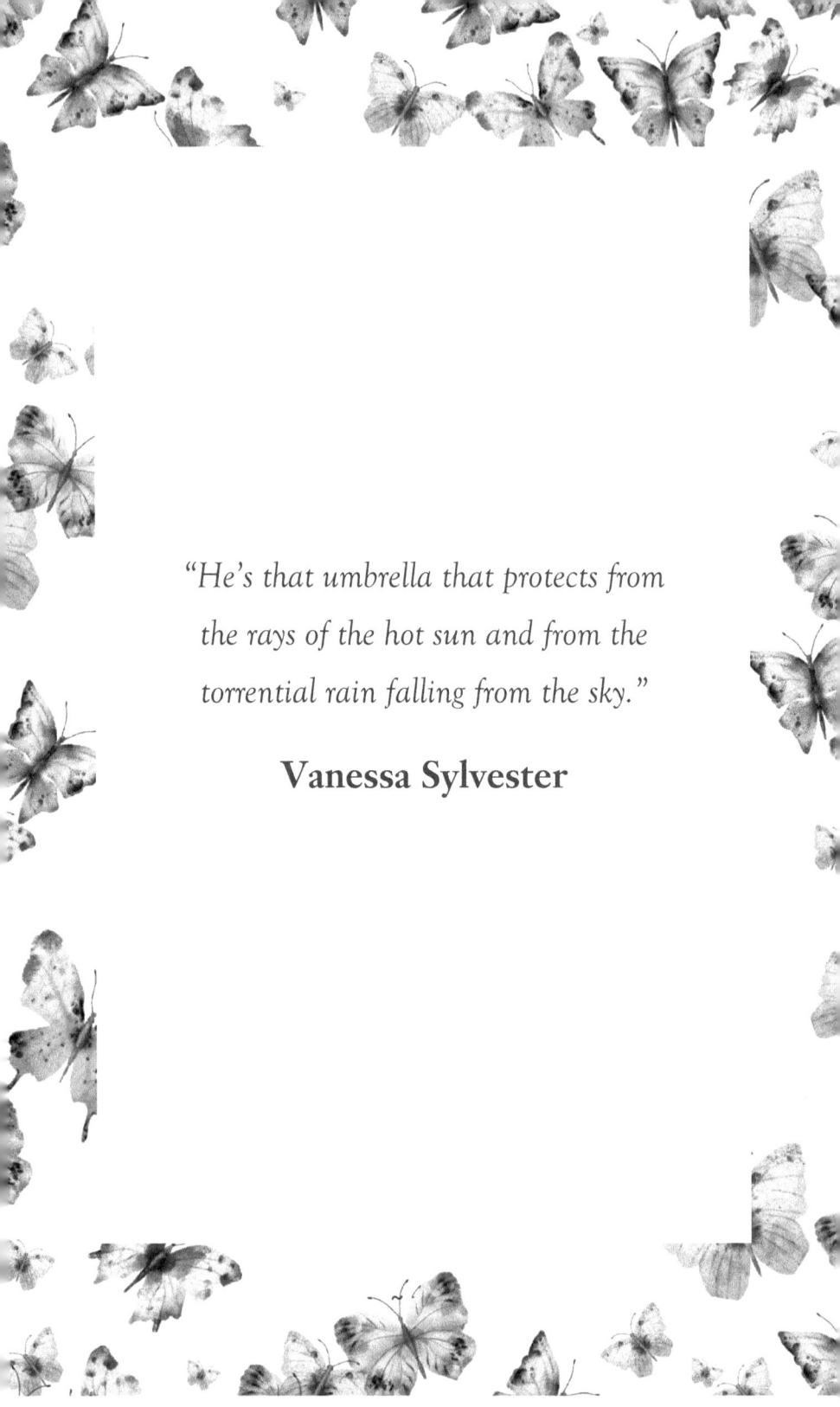

"He's that umbrella that protects from the rays of the hot sun and from the torrential rain falling from the sky."

Vanessa Sylvester

You are a
Butterfly4Jesus

www.ingramcontent.com/pod-product-compliance
Lightning Source LLC
Chambersburg PA
CBHW061225070526
44584CB00029B/3995